HOW TO PLAY THE
GAME OF COLLEGE!

By Dr. Shawn A. Boyd

TABLE OF CONTENTS

A NOTE TO PARENTS

Congratulations, mom, dad, grandma, grandpa, and the entire village!

We now have a high school senior who will soon leave high school and start a new chapter. I hope every young adult attending college is ready for a successful venture on day one.

However, many will arrive unprepared for the journey.

I wrote this book to equip the village with the necessary tools to establish a proper support system as your young adult navigates the murky waters and ventures into uncharted territory.

I can provide a few nuggets of wisdom for this journey:

1. Be a listening ear.
    Although he or she believes they know more than you, be that listening ear. Parents, times will arise when you want to jump in the driver's seat and steer the boat through the raging waters. Remember, this journey is not yours. Provide advice when necessary, but listening more will be more helpful.

2. Establish expectations.

Remember, many of you, as the parents, are financing your child's college education. So, why would you support subpar academic performance (i.e., failing grades)? Establish your expectations with them initially, and provide the consequences for unmet expectations. While some may believe employing consequences is harsh, you, the parents, are one of the main obstacles to students' success. I once heard a parent tell me she could not make her student do anything since he was alone in college. I asked her, "Do you pay any bills?" She said yes, the cell phone, car note, insurance, etc. I said, "So you have the power." Remember, parents, to set the expectations and ensure you follow through with consequences. We will explore expectations in greater detail in the first quarter.

3. It is okay not to know everything.

Many parents did not attend or complete college. If you are a college graduate, best practices and trends are constantly changing in higher education. Seek the knowledge, and ensure you include your child at every step. Remember, this is their college career. You are simply there to assist. When your child arrives on campus, there are parental boundaries you now have to follow, such as FERPA (Family Educational Rights and

Privacy Act), which protects your student's educational information, grades, etc., from everyone, including you.

4. Prepare for the unexpected.

   Before your child leaves for college, recall all the mischievous things you did as a child and multiply them by forty. Remember when I stated earlier your child would travel to uncharted territories? Sometimes uncharted territories are sex, drugs, parties, etc. However, you hold the map, so there is time to steer them on the right course by having those crucial conversations before they arrive on campus.

5. Repeat that they have your support—no matter what direction they steer the boat.

   Let them know that on their journey through this experience, you will always be in the boat. Parents, there will be some rough waters ahead, so get ready! I wish I could tell you that college will be a breeze. I would be lying. Sometimes, your child wants to drop out, or the grades are horrible. They may decide to postpone college and become a YouTube influencer. Yes, that is a thing; you must support your son or daughter's decision.

In conclusion, if you read this book with your child, you are already on the right path, as it will give you a foundation to support your child on this journey.

So again, parents, I pray for you as you embark on this journey with your son or daughter; building a support system is also essential. Many colleges offer parent associations.

Join them!

A NOTE TO EDUCATORS

Rita Pierson, a teacher for 40 years, once heard a colleague say, "They don't pay me to like the kids." Her response: "Kids don't learn from people they don't like."

This insight is a powerful call to teachers to believe in their students and connect with them on a relatable, human, and personal level. When I think of the many teachers who helped me become the man I am today, I cannot say thank you enough. When I think of the many roles you fulfill for students, there are not enough titles to capture them all. Some serve as parents, coaches, cheerleaders, bankers, motivators, and life coaches.

THANK YOU!

Although the compensation is lacking, your work means the world to the students you work with daily.

Thank you to all of the teachers in my life.

I dedicate this book to every teacher at my elementary school, Sharpe; my middle school, Colonial; and my high school, Overton. Those teachers poured so much into me, making me the scholar I am today.

A NOTE TO STUDENTS

You put a lot of hard work and sacrifice into getting to where you are now. Whether you are a high school junior or senior who is ending your high school career or a first-year student who has started college, this book is for you. I wish this manual had been available when I started college almost twenty years ago. I remember the millions of questions I asked, my concerns, my anxiety, and my nervousness about what was coming down the road.

So trust me, I get it!

College is very different from high school, and the students who get that will succeed. After reading the book and reflecting, you will be a professional college student, or at least look like a professional, when tackling the college transition and the many challenges it can sometimes bring.

Take a deep breath—you've got this!

Remember, you are the captain of this ship.

Congratulations again on making it this far in this journey called life.

11

Here are four quarters that will help you succeed at the game of college!

INTRODUCTION

My WHY!
I remember riding in the car with mom and often hearing Whitney Houston's song, *I Want to Dance with Somebody,* playing in the background. Yes, it was the 1980s. While taking me to school, she always said,

"I want you to go to college and make something of yourself."

See, my mom did not attend college. I am not sure how much it affected her, but she wanted me to have something she did not have: a bachelor's degree. Somehow she knew that the streets would become my college if I did not attend college. My mother also knew there were no shortcuts in life—you had to work hard for everything you wanted. And she taught me that hard work is what makes things happen.

Fast forward to my senior year of high school. I remember my guidance counselor, Mrs. Sonja Sanes. Mrs. Sanes had many outstanding qualities, but her impeccable style stood out to many people. Granted, Ms. Sanes was a guidance counselor, yet she dressed daily as though President Obama would visit.

13

Everyone respected Mrs. Sanes, and when she called, you answered.

I remember her calling me weekly to hear from and speak with college admissions representatives.

I would say to Mrs. Sanes, "Do I go?"

She would say, "Yes, sir!"

As I mentioned, I was a first-generation college student who did not know higher education's inner workings. All I knew was that my mom wanted me to attend, and my mother and I were unsure about funding this goal. Were it not for Mrs. Sanes' support, college would not be an option.

I was not in the top 10 percent of my class, and I didn't score a 30 on the ACT.

However, Mrs. Sanes made me feel like she cared, no matter my test score. So, with her guidance, I successfully gained admission into college and graduated with my bachelor's degree.

I loved college so much that it became my career. My first position was as a college recruiter at LeMoyne-Owen College, an HBCU in Memphis, TN. I wanted every student, no matter race, creed, or background, to have access to postsecondary education, and I knew that in my role as a recruiter, I could assist in making that goal a reality.

I'm lucky to be in a position where I can advocate for and change policy so that Tennessee students can earn post-secondary education credentials.

So, why a book?

This book is about college, and it is for everyone.

I wrote this book from a place of wisdom and love. It teaches parents, educators, and students that college is not only a possibility—it is their destiny.

Every person can be successful in college if they are willing to work hard, stay focused, and put their best foot forward as they take on new challenges.

College is a beautiful opportunity to grow into the person you want to become. You can learn more than just helpful information; you can discover who you are.

The world is changing quickly, and many of us feel overwhelmed by its pace. We are living in an age where we cannot rely on our parents' generation's advice to get us through life. We have to make our own decisions, and we have to prepare for those choices now.

However, what if you do not know how?

What if you do not have the skills or resources to figure out what you want to do with your life?

What if you do not know how to make good choices?

Well, fear not!

I have great news: this book is for people like you.

It is a guidebook that will help answer all those questions and more because it comes from a place of wisdom and love—my profession. It guides parents, educators, and students, showing them that college is a possibility and your destiny!

It is time for parents, students, and educators to start the game. Rest assured; you will win this game using this book as your guide.

FIRST QUARTER

MAKING A CHOICE TO BECOME A PROFESSIONAL COLLEGE STUDENT

C ongratulations!

You have chosen to attend college.

So now what?

First, take a deep breath and pause for a moment. Unbelievably, college goes by fast; many days, I look back at my three degrees and wonder where the time went.

Transitioning from high school to college can be challenging. Being a professional college student means that you are considered an adult and control your college career. For example, none of your teachers will call your mom if you miss English class.

Guess what?

It all falls on you!

18

So many thoughts were running through my mind the day I left home for college. I was nervous and excited as I prepared and loaded the car for the trip. As my mom drove, I was excited about setting up my dorm room with all the swag I had bought from Walmart. Conversely, I was also anxious about this new beginning and what it might bring.

So, no matter where you are on this journey, I have felt similar emotions and had the same thoughts. As you prepare to become a "real" or professional college student, I am sure the tips, advice, and information here will help you win.

Remember the importance of more than "book learning"

Before we get into the nitty-gritty of college, let us remember a few essential pointers. College is about new experiences, and not all occur in the classroom. This first quarter will cover tips to prepare you for college as you transition from high school to college.

If you are already in college, keep this book; do not put it down.

And if you're a parent making this transition, here are some pointers for your future college student.

1. Remind them that their relationships will change no matter who they are with during this time.

19

2. Repeat that they have your support, regardless of life's direction.
3. Equip them with knowledge concerning alcohol, drugs, sex, and other serious issues.
4. Provide only an agreed-upon sum of money, and only when necessary.
5. Discuss the future with real-world examples, so they focus on success.

Today's typical college experience is so vast that everyone will have a different one. Some of that is due to differences in personality, geographic location, or career interests, to name a few.

Parents, your influence over your child throughout their senior year of high school will change if they attend college. Understand that even the best parenting does not permanently save a child from challenges.

You can prepare your child for college, but it is up to them to succeed.

Okay, so let us get started and clear the air by reminding the people still on the fence why college is essential.

QUESTIONS ABOUT COLLEGE?

Why go to college?

College can help you learn new things and gain skills that will help you succeed in your career. If you are an educator or parent, I am sure you agree. Convincing a high school senior to consider the future can be challenging, but imparting good information is vital. Remember, education is becoming increasingly valuable each year, and those with higher education generally see the most success.

How do I choose a college?

So, parents and students have many factors to consider when choosing a college, including location, size, cost, academic programs, and campus culture. It would help if you also thought about whether you want to attend a public or private college and whether you want to stay in-state or go out-of-state. In the following section, I will detail the different types of institutions to help you determine which is best for you.

How do I apply to college?

Applying to college usually involves:

- completing an application form,
- submitting transcripts and test scores,
- writing an admission essay,
- providing letters of recommendation, and
- completing an interview.

How do I pay for college?

There are many options for paying for college, including scholarships, grants, loans, and work-study programs. However, it would help if you also considered the cost of tuition, room and board, and other expenses. Do not worry; we will discuss this subject in the fourth quarter.

What should I expect in college?

So, college is typically more academically challenging for students than high school. You must take a full course load, complete assignments, and exams, and meet academic standards. However, you will also have more freedom and independence than in high school.

How do you succeed in college?

To succeed in college, you will need to be self-motivated and organized. You should also develop good study habits, seek help, and get involved in campus life.

This book will help you answer these questions and so many more! Now that we have cleared the air on those questions, you may wonder if high school and college are that different.

Have you seen the television show *A Different World*?

Let me explain.

High school and college (what is the difference?)

So students, when you were in high school, you had parents and teachers who could get all up in your business, Which, at times, was a good thing.

I remember my senior year at Overton High School. I was taking Honors Algebra II from Mrs. Tessera Hardaway. I had a part-time job that allowed me to work many hours. At this time, I thought I could manage; however, my grades said otherwise. I remember Mrs. Hardaway calling my mom and telling her my grades were going downhill. My mom was shocked when she learned I worked almost 20 hours over my regular shift. My mom said,

"Oh no, son. The job has to go; school is the number one priority."

I was upset with Mrs. Hardway for a few weeks but quickly got over that when I saw the A's on my test.

Here is my point: a portion of your high school experiences consists of you attending every class daily. Additionally, teachers complete class attendance daily to ensure you are present, and if you are absent, parental contact ensues.

In college, this will not occur. Professors cannot call your parents because you are legally protected under FERPA (the Family Education Rights and Privacy Act), which protects the privacy of student education records.

As a professional college student, finding a good balance between work and school is up to you. Talk with your professor if you encounter any challenges in the course. Remember, you cannot rely on your mom or dad to come in and save the day. This is your college career; take control of it immediately!

College is different from high school, and it should be!

You are in a new environment to live, learn, and grow! So if you are a parent or future college student, I am sure you know someone who attended college. In the table below, jot down what you have noticed as differences between high school and college.

High School	College
1	
2	
3	
4	
5	
6	
7	
8	
9	
10	

Now that you have explored how these two spaces differ, let us explore what you can do to create a smooth transition. So, for my educators, parents, and high school seniors, I will provide some tips for those considering college.

Tips to help you transition from high school to college!

1. Start strong.

Yes, that is simple. Yet, as simple as it sounds, many people struggle with this concept. It is challenging to raise a GPA, but very easy to drop one. In addition, if obtaining a college degree were just another easy checkmark, everyone would be doing it. In high school, the law required you to attend a school, or your parents could face legal prosecution. Now the choice is all yours; mom and dad might think differently. Attending college is an option. So if you choose to follow, go hard or go home.

2. Identify the tools needed to help you succeed.

Think about a track star trying to win a race in ballet shoes. It just will not work. To succeed, you need all the necessary tools to help you get to the finish line.

3. Explore and recognize your passion.

An essential aspect a first-year college student should consider when choosing a major is following their passion. If you are still deciding what career to pursue, take classes in different majors to see what interests you. While certain professions have academic tracks that require students to start immediately (for example, pre-law or pre-medicine), most majors allow you to take courses in several disciplines. By taking classes in various subjects, you can learn about other fields and decide if you want to get a degree in one of them. Many factors will contribute to your success in college, including the type of college you choose to attend.

WHAT TYPE OF COLLEGE SHOULD I ATTEND?

S o you have chosen to attend college and are ready to draft the next play.

What is this play exactly?

What type of college should you attend?

That is a great question. So let us explore the different types of colleges, starting with the technical college.

Technical/Trade College

Technical colleges, also called vocational or trade schools, offer specialized training in a particular field or trade. Here are some pros and cons of attending a technical college:

Pros of attending a technical or trade school

- Specialized training: Technical colleges offer training in a particular field or trade, which can help students who want to go in a specific direction with their careers.

- Shorter programs: Technical college programs are often faster than traditional four-year college programs, allowing students to enter the workforce more quickly.
- Hands-on learning: Technical colleges often stress hands-on learning and give students real-world experience through internships or job shadowing.
- Lower cost: Technical colleges can be less expensive than four-year colleges, which can be a significant advantage for students who are paying for college or are concerned about student debt.

The cons of attending a technical or trade school

- Credits from technical colleges may not transfer to four-year colleges, which makes it harder for students to get a bachelor's degree if they decide to do so later.
- There are fewer career options with a technical college degree as with a four-year college degree because the programs are more specialized.
- Limited resources: Technical colleges may have fewer resources, such as libraries and extracurricular opportunities.

Community College

A community college awards and offers associate degrees that can be transferred to four-year colleges or universities after two years. They also offer professional training and certificate programs in technical fields like health care or information technology (IT). The average tuition at a community college is less than half the cost of attending some private universities, making them an affordable option for many students who want to attend school but cannot afford it.

Pros of attending a community college:

- Lower cost: Community colleges are generally less expensive than four-year colleges, which can be a significant advantage for students who are paying for college or are concerned about student debt.
- Flexibility: Community colleges often offer a wide range of classes, including evening and online options, which can be more flexible for students working or with other commitments.
- Transfer options: Many community colleges have agreements with four-year colleges that allow students to transfer credits and complete their bachelor's degree at a four-year college.

Cons of attending a community college:

- The main disadvantage of a two-year college is that only a few programs are offered, which may not be the best fit for some students. However, this can also be an advantage, as it forces students to choose their major early on and commit to it.
- Another disadvantage is the lack of housing available at these schools. Students who live at home or with their parents may find it challenging to make time for classwork while working or taking care of other responsibilities.

Four-Year College/University

A four-year college or university is a school that offers a four-year degree. A four-year college or university can be a public or private institution. The term "college" refers to all higher education institutions, but today it's used primarily in the US. A four-year college or university is a postsecondary institution that grants undergraduate and graduate degrees. Many of these institutions are known as liberal arts colleges because their curriculum emphasizes undergraduate study in the liberal arts and sciences.

Pros of attending a four-year college:

- More specialized programs: Four-year colleges often offer more specialized programs and majors, which can be an advantage for students with a clear idea of what they want to study.
- More resources: Four-year colleges usually have more resources, like libraries, labs, and extracurricular activities, which can help students do better in school and make more friends.
- Degrees with more prestige: Four-year colleges tend to have a better reputation and can offer degrees with more prestige, which can help when applying for jobs or graduate school.

The cons of attending a four-year college

- First, many institutions require you to stay on campus for your studies. This requirement can be a disadvantage if you feel you need more independence or want to experience life off campus.
- In addition, out-of-state tuition can be significantly higher than in-state tuition at many institutions. This cost will cause your expenses to increase even more if you choose to attend an institution outside your home state or city.

- Finally, most four-year colleges require students to take out loans for funding purposes. While this is not always true for every institution, it is generally a good idea for students who plan on attending one of these schools within their first two years of college (before they enter graduate school).

Choosing the best college for you is an important decision that will likely impact your academic and professional careers. When choosing a college, thinking carefully about your goals, interests, and budget is important. Some factors to consider during your search include the following:

- The college's location
- The size of the school
- The cost of tuition and other expenses
- The academic programs offered
- The campus culture

You should also look into the college's reputation and consider job and graduate school options for graduates. Ultimately, the best college for you is the one that aligns with your goals and provides the resources and supports you need to succeed. Your communication will change as you decide to attend college, especially if it is a four-year college and you reside on campus.

Nine Actions to Master Before You Attend College

If you want to be a successful and independent college student, there are some behaviors you should adopt before starting college. Although these skills may seem basic, even some of my friends (whom I will not name) struggled with them.

1. Learn how to do laundry, including properly sorting, washing, and drying clothes.

2. Keep your living space clean and sanitized to avoid spreading germs and illness.

3. Develop basic clothing maintenance skills such as ironing and sewing on a button.

4. Learn how to manage your money by opening a checking and savings account, making a budget, and steering clear of credit cards.

5. Register to vote and participate in the democratic process.

6. Know how to send a package through the mail to send and receive items.

7. Keep your living space clean by regularly sweeping and mopping the floors.

8. Learn to cook at least three nutritious meals to fuel your body and save money.

8. Develop grocery shopping skills, including planning, comparison shopping, and making healthy choices.

9. Take responsibility for waking up on time by setting your alarm and not relying on others.

Communication with Family and Friends

I always advise the parents and students to sit down and discuss expectations before their student starts college.

First, it is critical to discuss financial expectations., such as agreeing on what bills the parents will pay or if you, the student, will seek part-time employment to reduce tuition costs.

Another expectation to discuss before enrollment is academic performance and expectations. Many college students make the erroneous decision to reveal their academic difficulties to their parents when they fail classes or withdraw prematurely and owe fees. You should determine what and how often you want to share your academic progress with your parents or guardians. You do not want your parents to be surprised about everything, especially if they are helping you financially to attend.

Now that expectations are established, students should remember that although they may be leaving home, they still need the support of their friends and family. So be open and honest with your family about your experiences and any challenges you may be facing. You can strengthen your relationships with your family and get the help you need in college if you talk to them often and stay in touch.

Remember, being in college is not only about you; your family is also essential. Your family and friends have spent much time in every aspect of your life. Remember, their love and care will not turn off automatically once you leave for school. Instead, try to include them as much as possible. I remember inviting my family to family days on campus, my fraternity step shows, or simply bringing them home a school t-shirt; small gestures of this nature made their day.

As much as you would like to believe you are Mr. or Ms. Independent, you will still need them!

Even if you are busy with course assignments and other responsibilities, setting aside time for communication and staying in touch is essential. Keeping in touch with family while in college is vital for keeping relationships strong and helping each other through this time of change.

There are several ways to stay in touch with family while at college, including phone calls, text messaging, video calls, and social media. Use technology to communicate with families, such as social media, emails, or face-to-face chat.

I also suggest sharing your schedule for classes and working with them. Hopefully, they will avoid tempting you to call during those critical times. It is also a good idea to schedule times to talk.

In closing, please keep in mind this key point: the importance of setting expectations now. The most important element to consider when setting expectations and goals is whether they are achievable. Setting goals is the best way to ensure your goals are attainable. This strategy will help you stay on track and prevent any setbacks from derailing your progress, so let us explore goal setting.

GOAL SETTING

Trust me, college will get tough, and you should not stop and throw in the towel.

It is so important to start with the end in mind!

Where do you see yourself after college in four to five years? Have you set your goals by "starting with the end in mind?"

People who set goals, long-term aims, or tasks to complete start by thinking about what they want to achieve in a given time frame and start working backward to formulate a plan for accomplishment.

It is necessary to write those goals out so they can be a constant reminder of why you are taking this journey called college.

These goals are all about you!

Setting goals means determining your goals, achievements, and values and writing them down. By making goals clear and specific, you show that you are committed to them and that they are yours. Ask yourself if your goals are consistent with your characteristics, abilities, and level of determination.

Sometimes, putting pen to paper helps clarify our thoughts about what we want to achieve. This exercise will help you set goals as a first-time college student, but it may also be helpful at other times in your life! Post these goals on your bathroom mirror or your closet door. Look at them often! This process will remind you why you are in college and the steps to achieving your goals. Goal setting is essential for college students to develop, as it can help them stay focused and motivated and achieve their academic and personal goals.

Seven ways goal setting helps in your college journey

Setting goals provides a clear path to success.

Setting goals will give you a clear path to your destination. It also alerts you when you venture off the path. Think about a goal the same way you think about the GPS in your car. You enter the address, and the GPS tells you how to get there step by step. The GPS is so specific that it notifies you when you will arrive. The unique thing about the GPS is that it tells you how to avoid traffic (i.e., pitfalls). It reroutes you so that you can make it to your destination safely. Nevertheless, just like the GPS, it is up to you to listen and follow the path that it is taking you.

Goals teach time management and preparedness.

Goals prepare you to plan for the worst but expect the best. Life will happen, but successful people are always ready for the worst. It is like having a supply of food, a flashlight, and candles; when a storm hits, you can survive for a few days. I am not implying it will be easy, but staying ready to take advantage of significant opportunities is always important.

Goals increase motivation.

I do not know about you, but I am competitive. When I set a goal, I am so motivated to reach it. I acquire tunnel vision and tune out everything around me. Most of my accomplishments started with a goal I was motivated to achieve. From pledging my fraternity to obtaining a doctorate and everything in between, my motivation to achieve the goal ensured it was accomplished.

Goals measure progress.

Goal setting is a process that helps us get the most out of our lives and careers. It is essential to set goals that are achievable but also challenging enough to make us feel like we are growing. Long-term goals are critical because they give you something to work towards in the future, but short-term goals help you stay focused on what is immediately in front of you. If you aim for a big dream and need to set up smaller ones along the way, you may lose sight of what is essential and lose motivation before getting close to your final destination.

One way to ensure adequate goal-setting works is by setting up deadlines. Deadlines are significant because they keep us from procrastinating indefinitely. Of course, you might find yourself changing paths to reach your goals—that is okay! Do not let yourself feel guilty about taking detours or working on other things along the way; keep an eye on where things are going so you can stay on track!

Goals give focus and purpose.

When you started reading this book, I wrote a letter to my readers, but more importantly, to myself: MY, WHY! It is why I wake up every day and feel motivated to do what I do in life. You have to remind yourself of your WHY constantly! Especially when you get tired or do not want to leave the bed. That is why she will push you to do the opposite.

Goals increase self-confidence.

When I started working out, I set goals regarding my weight loss or what I was lifting on the rack. When I began to see small results or started lifting heavier, I was like, "Hell yeah." Those results motivated me to continue on my journey.

Goals provide challenges.

Let me repeat: Nothing in life will come to you quickly. It would be best if you put in that work. I wish I could say being in college would come easily. It will not! However, if I did, you could do it, and matter of fact, better than me!

Accomplishing your goals is a fulfilling and empowering experience. It can provide satisfaction and achievement and motivate you to set and pursue new goals. When you achieve your goals, it is vital to take a moment to celebrate your success and reflect on what you have learned. This recognition can help you build confidence and momentum and provide valuable insights for future goals.

Being flexible and adaptable when you accomplish your goals is also essential. Reaching one goal may lead to new opportunities or challenges, and you may need to adjust your plans or set new goals accordingly. By staying open to change and embracing new opportunities, you can continue to grow and learn as you pursue your goals.

Overall, reaching your goals is a rewarding experience that can make you feel good and give you a sense of accomplishment. It can also encourage you to set and pursue new goals. So, it is important to celebrate your successes and stay open to new opportunities as you work toward your goals.

Mapping out your goals.

You have probably heard the phrase, "Don't let your goals be dreams," because it is easy for them to slip away from you when you do not know what you are setting out to do. When you map out your goals, you can ensure they are specific and know what you want to accomplish. This action will help keep them focused during the long journey toward achieving them so that it does not feel like a surprise when they reach the finish line. So, I have a mini-goal guide below to help you chart your short- and long-term goals.

My long-range goals to complete in the next 2-3 years:

1

2

3

The steps I need to take to achieve these (long-range) goals:

1

2

3

My (mid-range) goals to complete in the next year:

1

2

3

The steps I need to take to achieve these (mid-range) goals:

1

2

3

My (short-range) goals to complete by the first day of the semester:

1

2

3

The steps I need to take to achieve these (short-range) goals:

1

2

3

My (immediate) goals for the next month:

1

2

3

The steps I need to take to achieve these (immediate) goals:

1

2

3

Accomplishing goals is a task many people struggle with, so you are not alone. There are so many distractions and obstacles in our lives that it takes time to focus on what we want to accomplish and how we will get there. However, anything is possible if you are willing to plan your goals and follow through with the necessary steps.

As I listed above, planning your goals is the key.

First, you must be specific about what you want to achieve and how to get there. It might seem like much work at first, but once you start seeing results, it will be worth every minute spent planning what needs to happen next!

Now comes the hard part: following through with those plans! This action may not always be easy; it will take some self-discipline and a lot of dedication. However, as long as you're willing to put in the effort necessary to make it work, anything is possible! Now, when meeting goals in college, some specific "do's" and "don'ts" will help you accomplish them.

DO'S AND DON'TS

I have worked in higher education for over 12 years, and I have worked with some of the best and brightest and others who were on the verge of dropping out. Below, you will find some tips from several of my former students that helped them succeed in college and some tough lessons learned. Pay close attention and, by any means, avoid these pitfalls.

Do organize.

As a first-year student, you will face many challenges in your life. To meet these challenges head-on, you must become organized, hence the need for an online or physical planner.

For example, your first semester will be very hard because you must finish many assignments and projects on time. In addition, many classes require a lot of reading and writing, which can be challenging if you do not have a planner or schedule. Additionally, your classes are held at different times every week, making planning for these assignments and projects even harder. As a result, it is easy to forget an assignment or project because of the lack of organization in your life.

Another option is an accountability partner.

Having an accountability partner will help you stay on track with all your coursework and other activities outside the classroom, such as working part-time jobs or volunteering at local organizations in your community. This option will allow you to hold each other accountable when someone misses something important, such as submitting an assignment on time or regularly attending meetings.

Do go to office hours.

Professors are intimidating. They are intelligent, successful, and have a lot of experience. However, if you think that means you should keep your distance from them, you could not be more wrong.

The key to getting the most out of your education is to build a positive relationship with your professors because they can help you maximize your experience. Professors know what will make you successful in your courses and life after college. They also have connections and resources to help you succeed beyond the classroom. So do not be afraid to reach out!

You might assume that because they are busy or seem intimidating, it would be better to wait until they approach you with questions about your academic progress rather than taking the initiative yourself.

However, this is a mistake. If something important needs to be discussed with a professor (like how well you are doing in their class), it is always better for both parties if it happens sooner rather than later. This approach can help you avoid any unpleasant surprises later on!

Do go out and meet people.

College is a time in your life when you learn about yourself and grow as a person. It is also a great time to build relationships with other people. The best way to succeed in college is by joining organizations and attending events hosted by them.

First, joining an organization can help you meet new people and make friends who share your interests. Surrounding yourself with positive people who support you when you need it most is essential.

Second, joining an organization allows you to learn more about yourself and your interests. You might discover something new about yourself that could change the direction of your career path!

Lastly, joining an organization helps you become a better leader by allowing you to take on new responsibilities and care for the well-being of others. Moreover, it will prepare you for entering the workforce after graduation! Do not worry; we will discuss campus involvement later this quarter.

Do make time to exercise.

Physical wellness is essential for all of us, as it helps us stay healthy and maintain a good quality of life. As a first-year student in college, it can be challenging to find the time to prioritize physical activity, but it is worth it to prioritize your physical health.

College students must take care of their bodies as they are often more stressed because of school, relationships, and financial stress. The demands on your time are high at this stage in life, and you often need the resources or support network you had before enrolling in college.

By staying active, you reduce stress and improve your mood. More importantly, you will have more energy and less trouble sleeping at night. Keeping busy can relieve some of these stressors by allowing you to move your body and meet people who like the same things you do.

Do use campus resources.

It is okay to feel overwhelmed in college.

I know how it feels to be a freshman and feel like the world has suddenly opened before you. It is like being thrown into an ocean and told to swim for your life. You are expected to make friends, study for classes, find your way around campus, and learn how to get meals without spending all your money. You are supposed to do all this while managing your feelings about leaving home, adjusting to a new environment, and figuring out who you are as an adult.

What if I told you there are resources on campus that can help?

What if I told you some people want to help you manage the emotional and psychological stress and anxiety of being a college student?

What if I told you these resources exist so they can help you?

Your university will provide many resources. Some resources assist students who feel academically overwhelmed and struggle with writing. There are resources for students who are stressed because they have too much work or who just need someone who understands what it means to be 18 years old with no idea where their life is going next.

Do attend class regularly.

Regularly attending class can help you stay on track and maximize your education.

Do seek help when needed.

Be bold and ask for help when you need it, whether it is from professors, tutors, or academic advisors.

Don't stay in your room and hide.

Building relationships with peers is one of the essential parts of college. It is also one of the most challenging because you are not just meeting new people; you are meeting new people in a new place!

Your residence hall is a great place to start. You will meet other students with similar experiences, and if you take advantage of opportunities to get involved, you will likely make lifelong friends.

If you need more confidence or are trying to figure out where to start, there are many ways to get out of your room and into the heart of student life on campus. The first step is the easiest: join an organization based on your interests and hobbies. If it does not interest you right now, try it out anyway.

The second step is more complex: leave your room!

Remember that every time you return from winter break or summer vacation, there will be new faces around campus—faces that might become good friends if only they knew who was behind door #1 (or even #2).

So go out there and meet people.

Don't procrastinate.

Earlier in the book, I mentioned that college is a great time to get organized. I wanted to talk about how important it is to plan and avoid procrastinating.

When you are in high school, deadlines are more relaxed than deadlines for academic assignments in college. In high school, you have more time to do your work and redo it if necessary. In college, professors are less sympathetic with their deadlines, so even though you may not be able to get something perfect on the first try, it is essential to plan so that when finals arrive, you do not have to scramble for ideas.

If you want your college experience to be good, set aside some time every week to plan what needs completing and when (before it becomes too late). The result is fewer surprises and more time to relax.

Don't overschedule yourself.

It is easy to feel overwhelmed as a freshman. There are many activities, so much to do, and many people to meet. It is tempting to go into overdrive, trying to get involved in everything possible.

Nevertheless, do not let yourself be overwhelmed! You will not be able to take on every opportunity that comes your way, and you certainly want your first week at college to be manageable!

Instead, try this:

- Move with ease. If you want to spread yourself too thin or feel like you have too much on your plate, step back and work on moving with ease.
- Take a breath and remind yourself that it is okay if there are some activities you pursue at a later date; there will always be more opportunities down the road.
- And if something makes you uncomfortable because it does not feel right, let it go! There are plenty of other things out there waiting for you.
- Do not overwhelm yourself. You are only just beginning what will hopefully be one of the best journeys of your life!

Don't study for 20 minutes and expect to know the material.

College-level academics are indeed more challenging than high school classes. However, this does not mean you "wing it" and hope for the best. To succeed in college, you need to make studying a priority. The first step is to stop thinking of studying as memorizing information and start thinking of it as contextualizing details.

When we study, we learn how things fit together—how they are connected, what they have in common, and where they differ. In other words, we do not just memorize facts.

Don't be afraid to try new things.

College is a time to explore and try new things. Do not hesitate to step outside your comfort zone and try new activities and experiences.

In conclusion, these are just a few "dos" and "don'ts" for a college student. By following these guidelines and using good judgment, you can set yourself up for success in college and beyond.

Now, one "do" I forgot to mention, which is an experience I highly recommend, is living with a roommate. If you are like me, you love your space. Having a college roommate can be a fantastic experience. Not only do you have someone to talk to when you come back to your room late at night or after a long day of classes, but you also have someone there to help keep you accountable for studying and doing your homework.

It might be hard to know what to expect if you have never had a roommate. So let us discuss how you can make this experience unforgettable.

CONNECTING WITH YOUR COLLEGE ROOMMATE

Getting off to a good start with your college roommate can help make your college experience much happier.

I can count, over the years, the many times I had to help roommates figure out how to live peacefully in a shared living space. So keep these tips in mind to ensure your new home is peaceful.

The key point to remember is that I do not suggest going into this experience to make a new best friend; instead, try to be the best roommate.

Sharing a room with a college roommate can be a wonderful experience. It can be an opportunity to make a new friend, learn to live with someone else, and save money on housing. However, it can also be challenging at times. Here are a few tips for making the most of your college roommate experience:

Steps to Take Before Arriving on Campus:

1. Call your future roommate to get acquainted. Most colleges and universities will notify you in advance of who your new roommate will be. Often, the college will give you the contact information for your roommate. Call them, introduce yourself, and tell them you look forward to meeting them in person.

2. Use social networks to stay in touch. Review their profile on Facebook or other social networking sites. You may learn helpful information, such as their preferences, interests, and hobbies develop a sense of their personality. If you feel comfortable doing so, invite them to join your network.

3. Exchange photos. If you find it difficult to talk with someone you have yet to meet, sending them pictures of your friends, places you have traveled, and neighborhood hangouts may be a great way to establish a connection.

4. Establish responsibility: I suggest you call the college residence hall to obtain the suggested packing list, room layout, and square footage of your room. I remember a student who brought an entire 50-gallon fish tank with fish, only to find out when she unpacked the institution prohibited pets in the dorm room.

Steps to Take While You're Sharing a Dorm Room:

Do you know the feeling of being in a new place where you do not know anyone?

It is the worst.

What if I told you that your roommate could mitigate this feeling?

Sure, it is not like they can hold your hand through life's ups and downs, but they can make things a little easier on you—and even help you meet new people. Sharing a dorm room with a roommate can be a great way to meet new people and make friends. It can also be a horrible, awful experience that leaves you wishing you were back in your room at home. Here are some tips to help you maximize your shared space:

- **Communicate.** The most critical factor in any roommate situation is to communicate constructively. Even if you socialize in different circles, try exchanging daily pleasantries. Always be courteous and respectful.
- **Address conflicts directly and tactfully.** Creating a friendly atmosphere will make it easier to discuss the inevitable disagreements.

- **Establish the basic house rules.** Avoid significant conflicts by developing mutually agreeable house rules and expectations regarding cleanliness, study hours, and guests.
- **Be willing to compromise.** Sharing a tiny dorm room requires some tolerance and a willingness to compromise. Speak up when you must, but strive to accommodate personal differences that do not impact your safety or well-being.
- **Be sensitive to different financial situations.** You and your new roommate may come from very different backgrounds. Help each other feel comfortable by proposing social activities that will not create an excessive financial burden.
- **Respect each other's property.** Treat your roommate's property with at least as much consideration as yours. Ask before borrowing anything. Hold yourself responsible for anything your guests use or damage if you invite them into your shared space.
- **Get outside help if needed.** Many colleges and universities will ask you to wait until the end of the semester before reassigning roommates. It is a great life practice to learn to get along. However, if you see signs of serious issues like an eating disorder or substance abuse, it is wise to consult a trusted

older adult rather than try to handle it yourself.

Even if you are complete opposites, you can be cordial and provide each other with mutual support. You may even wind up becoming lifelong friends. Common sense and courtesy will help you and your new roommate get along.

Resident Assistants and Resident Directors.

Remember, your resident assistant and resident director will be great resources if you encounter residential or dorm life issues. Feel free to reach out to them. Most are available 24 hours a day. Resident assistants are trained to help first-year students adjust to their new environment and often serve as peer mentors. Their presence in the residence halls, or dorms, reminded me of the many different types of mentoring available to students and how important it is for college students to embrace mentorship at every level.

MENTORSHIP
MATTERS

Coll... ollege students often enter new and unfamiliar territory, making them feel alone. However, some people, such as mentors, can help you. You may need to learn how to approach professors, start a research project, or manage workloads. Mentors can help you navigate these uncharted territories by guiding you through learning new skills.

Trust me; I have several mentors. I can pick up the phone and ask for advice about personal things in my life and career.

I want to dedicate this chapter to my mentors, who have helped make me the man that folks see in front of them today. My mentors have seen the best and worst in me. Thank you to each of you who have stood by me from the beginning. A mentor is invaluable for several reasons:

Six Advantages of Having a Mentor

1.) Mentors have walked the path. They can answer questions others cannot.

Mentors are not just helpful; they are indispensable. They have been where you want to go, so they know what it takes to get there. They have learned from their mistakes and know how to avoid making them again. They have a wealth of knowledge and experience and want to share it with you. A mentor can help you figure out where to start, what questions to ask yourself, and how to ensure a successful journey.

2.) Mentors can help with your long-range and short-term goals.

A mentor has traveled the path you are embarking upon and wants to help you get there. More importantly, he or she can guide you on how to get there. Mentors are great for providing advice on long-term goals but can also help with short-term goals. For example, you may need help planning a project or preparing for an interview. A mentor can guide you on the best way to structure the project and possible questions you should propose during the interview.

3.) Mentors can help you develop the necessary skills.

Mentors are there to help you learn and grow in your chosen field, and they can also give feedback on what you are doing right and ways to improve. When I started my career, I had a mentor who helped me understand how to use the tools available. She also gave me great advice about my work ethic, which helped me grow as a worker.

4.) Mentors can give you access to their contacts.

Networking (which we will explore in the second quarter) is invaluable, and a mentor can help you navigate your industry and contact the right people. They can introduce you to others in their network to help you make connections. Mentors also understand current industry trends and recruitment practices and can offer introductions to individuals who can assist you.

5.) A mentor-sponsored opinion

Mentors have many roles in the lives of their mentees, but they are all based on a straightforward principle: an unbiased perspective. Mentors are there to be a sounding board for their mentees, and their opinions or biases should not sway them. Whether it is a parent or a teacher, a mentor has a similar lived experience as the mentee that only comes from experience.

6.) Mentors have connections to opportunities.

In the world of business, a mentor is someone who teaches you how to be successful. They have connections to opportunities, and they share their knowledge and experience with you so that you can grow your career.

Mentors can help you build your confidence, ensure you are on the right path, and teach you how to succeed in your career. They can help guide you when times get tough and offer advice when needed.

Finding the Right Mentor

Having a mentor has many benefits! However, the obvious question is, "How do I find a mentor?"

Try these strategies:

1. Identify a mentor.

Identifying a mentor can be challenging, especially if you are just getting started in your field or are new to it. An excellent first step is to identify someone already in your field, but not necessarily your boss or the person who hired you. Connecting with people outside your immediate circle is often easier because those relationships might not be as fraught with politics or questions about how much time you spend on a project.

Start with someone who can help you grow professionally, and then ask them if they could talk over lunch or coffee sometime soon. There is no need to come right out and ask them if they will be your mentor. Simply ask that you would like to get their advice on some things related to your prospective profession, like what classes or certifications might help you advance in this area or where else you could network with other professionals in the field.

2. Research online.

Some websites connect mentors with those looking for a mentor. One such example is www.findamentor.com. You can find mentors who specialize in the same field as you or who are not in your field. If you want a career-specific mentor, search for someone with a similar job title or role.

If you are looking for a mentor who specializes in something different from your work experience, search for someone whose background is similar to yours (for example, if they went to the same school or have similar hobbies).

For example, if you currently work as an accountant at a company and want to become a project manager, research accountants who have become project managers at that company. Find out what training or skills are needed to decide if the path is worth exploring.

You can also use online tools like LinkedIn's "Find People" feature to find potential mentors based on their education and job titles.

3. Communicate your level of commitment.

For me, the mentor-mentee relationship is a two-way street. You can only be successful if you are willing to work, which means both parties must be committed to each other. The mentor needs to take their mentee seriously, and the mentee needs to be honest about what they want out of the relationship and how they plan on getting there.

Finding a mentor will allow you to achieve success quickly and smoothly. A mentor will help you take advantage of the best opportunities, avoid speed bumps, and become more involved on campus. This brings us to the next topic, campus involvement.

THE IMPORTANCE OF CAMPUS INVOLVEMENT

"Getting involved on campus has been one of the most rewarding experiences of my college career. I've met so many amazing people, gained valuable leadership skills, and learned so much about myself and what I'm passionate about. I highly encourage all college students to get involved and make the most of their college experience."

Brian Hall, college student

A significant component of your collegiate experience happens outside the classroom. If you think about it, you will spend more time outside the classroom than in class. You should get to know your campus, where classes are, and the various student involvement offices.

So here are some tips to remember:

1. Make friends.

Making friends in college can be a challenge. You are not just making friends; you are building a tribe.

So, finding people who share your interests, values, and sense of humor is essential.

First, start by finding people who are into the same things you are. If you are into sports and your new friend is not, they might be more interested in something else, like music or movies.

Next, consider whether or not this person shares your values. It might be hard for the friendship to progress if they do not. For example, if someone does not share your love of dogs and cats, engaging with them is probably no point because they will not understand why you always must bring your pet along when visiting their house or apartment.

Finally, look for people who share your sense of humor! You do not have to be best friends with everyone—find one person who makes you laugh and enjoy hanging out with them because they make life feel lighter and brighter when they are around.

2. Feel part of a community.

Although I knew a few people from my hometown when I first came to college, I was a freshman and slightly nervous about starting this new life. The first thing I did was find a community.

Finding my community was one of the most helpful things I could have done when starting college. It made me feel more comfortable and confident in my new surroundings.

So how do you find your community?

Well, it will be different for everyone, but one thing you can do is go out and explore! Make sure you check out all the different clubs, student organizations, and activities that are available on campus. You never know what might catch your attention until you look around.

3. Expand interests.

As a college freshman, you may feel like the world is at your fingertips. You have all the freedom and an entire campus full of people like you—impossibly exciting and fun. You might feel like there is no way to run out of things to do or that nothing could push you outside of your comfort zone.

However, here is the thing: You are wrong!

If you want to make sure that your time at college is genuinely transformative, then it is time for you to start pushing yourself outside of your comfort zone. All kinds of activities on campus can help with this, including clubs and sports teams, but we would like to suggest something else: volunteering! Not only will it help you connect with people from different walks of life than yourself, but it will also give you a chance to use your skills in service of others, a skill that will stay with you for life.

4. Have fun while saving money.

Saving money as a college student is challenging. Between tuition and textbooks, it is easy to feel overwhelmed by all the costs and forget about the fun things in life.

However, there are ways to get out of your dorm room and save money. Here are some ideas:

- Attend free events on campus. There are many events on campus daily, and they are always free! You can attend open mics, lectures from visiting professors, or even hang out with friends at the library.
- Attend off-campus activities that offer discounts. Even if you are not into sports or clubs, there are plenty of ways to get discounts on off-campus activities with your student ID card—like going to the movies or local restaurants!
- Research study abroad opportunities. If you want to travel but cannot afford it yet, your university can assist with this goal. You can go abroad for less than it would cost here in America and still get school credit!

5. Future employers are interested in soft skills.

College is the time to hone the skills that employers are seeking. One way to do this is to join a student organization, which can help you develop leadership skills and strengthen your soft skills.

As a college student, you have plenty of opportunities to develop your leadership skills. You can lead projects for your class, volunteer at a local organization, or even run for student office. These experiences will allow you to show off your organizational skills and ability to manage other people's schedules and deadlines.

Soft skills are also crucial for employers but are often overlooked in favor of more complex skills. Soft skills include communication and problem-solving abilities—skills that may not come naturally to everyone but are just as important!

Student organizations are great places to practice these soft skills in a low-pressure environment where you will not feel like anyone is watching or judging you. They also allow you to meet other students who share similar interests; this can help build lasting relationships with people who could be valuable connections later in life!

6. Create a network with little effort.

One of the most important things you can do as a college student is to build your network.

Having connections with people outside of your school can help you find out about opportunities and resources that are not available on campus. You may not realize it, but there are many opportunities—you need someone to tell you about them!

Just think: what would happen if you had access to all the connections around you and all the knowledge those connections contain? What could you accomplish? With this in mind, start connecting with people outside your institution today!

7. Last but not least, statistics show that involvement improves student success. Students active in student organizations are more likely to feel connected to the institution and complete their degree.

So the college has a student involvement fair with free food, music, and entertainment.

GO!!!!

Please stop by the various tables to learn more about the different organizations. Every campus will showcase its student organizations. Most students lead these groups and usually have a staff or faculty member as the advisor. Although the organizations have an advisor, the students are running the show, everything from learning to leading meetings, creating budgets, writing proposals, and organizing huge events.

So, if for a moment you are questioning whether you should join a student organization, stop questioning,

DO IT!!!

Now, I can see your point that joining an organization takes time and energy, and you need to focus on school first.

Excellent point, and please consider the following:

Being in an organization is like having a small family network. Additionally, organizations often have a GPA requirement, so this supports your academic goals. Many organizations offer their members study sessions and tutoring. Plus, you get that sense of belonging. Many of you will attend large universities, and losing your way is easy. Being an active member of an organization shrinks the college down to size and helps you feel like you belong and have a family around you to check on you during some of those low moments you will endure.

Types of Involvement

Although numerous extracurricular activities exist, the following are most commonly found on college campuses:

1. Student Government Association
2. Athletics
3. Intramural Sports
4. Academic and professional organizations
5. Volunteer and service-related activities
6. Multicultural Activities.
7. The Arts

8. Greek Organizations
9. Faith/Spiritual Organizations

Write down three to five organizations you want to explore and how you plan to research them. If you ever want to try something new, this is the time to do so.

I remember wanting to learn chess and joining the chess club. This decision did not work out well for me! However, this was a great decision because I learned that if you do not like something, try the next thing until you find what you want.

The main goal is to try something, so I suggest taking full advantage of your first year in college and discovering your passions through clubs and organizations.

Below, after you visit the involvement fair, write down at least five organizations you would like to research more! Throw in one that is new to you that you would like to try!

- **Organization 1**

- **Organization 2**

- **Organization 3**

- **Organization 4**

- **Organization 5**

I remember looking back at my freshman year and joining the freshman forum at MTSU. In that organization, I met some friends I am still in touch with almost 20 years later. I later joined a Greek organization, Kappa Alpha Psi Fraternity, Inc. I served in several leadership positions, took several free trips sponsored by my fraternity, and developed a lifelong bond with my brothers.

Now that I have mentioned Greek life let us explore this experience.

To pledge or not to pledge?

Whether or not you want to join a fraternity or sorority is a personal choice you should make on your own. Joining a fraternity or sorority can be a rewarding experience that can lead to leadership, community service, and friendships that last a lifetime. However, it can also be time-consuming and expensive and may not be the right fit for everyone.

Here are a few things to consider if you consider pledging:

- Research the fraternity or sorority culture and values. Make sure the organization aligns with your values and goals.
- Understand the time and financial commitments. Membership can be a significant time investment, and there may be fees associated with membership.
- Talk to current members and alumni. Ask them about their experiences and whether they believe it was worth the time and money.
- Consider your priorities and schedule. Ensure you have enough time to devote to your academics and other activities.

Nearly 9 million college students have decided to join a sorority or fraternity. I would advise anyone seeking to join Greek life to get involved in other organizations first. Many campuses do not allow students to join a Greek organization their first semester, and many black Greek-lettered organizations do not allow membership until after a student's first year. Also, many are selective, and you must undergo a strenuous interview to join.

What better way to get practice and experience than by joining other organizations?

I will go into more detail in my second book about Greek life. Stay tuned. Shameless plug. ☺ Ultimately, the decision to pledge or not to pledge should be based on what is best for you and your individual goals and priorities. It is essential to do your research and make an informed decision.

So, as I close this section, I want you to know that membership in every organization is impossible. Healthy involvement is critical, but please do not overdo it. Involvement also means going to the various programs on campus, especially those that you are least experienced with, so you can appreciate all your campus has to offer. Too often, I see students focused more on involvement than coursework; remember that your schoolwork comes before any organization. An organization should support what is happening in the classroom, not compete with it!

FIRST QUARTER RECAP

S o we started this quarter with a bang and covered a lot of material. As I previously stated, the decision to attend college is significant. It is the start of your next chapter, an opportunity to meet new people, learn new things, and grow as a person because high school and college are very different. Students must navigate through classes, roommates, friendships, and even the first taste of independence at home. Parents, this initial encounter is when students learn how to manage their time and set goals for themselves. They also learn about communication skills and how to deal with people different from them, and this often comes through living on campus with a roommate and having a mentor. Colleges provide many opportunities for students to become involved in campus activities that can help them grow personally and professionally.

SECOND QUARTER

CHOOSING A MAJOR

The number one question I am sure you are asking yourself is,

"What do I want to do for a lifetime?"

I am confident you often ponder this question and are often asked by friends and family.

So I am no different.

What is your major?

With so many choices and options, this question needs to be clarified. So explore the following what-if scenario and jot down the thoughts that come immediately to your mind.

What if Oprah Winfrey were your godmother, and her final gift to you was the opportunity to turn your passion into your life's work? Money is not an issue, and you have access to any training, education, or educational experience you desire. What kind of career would you pursue?

List 1–3 options here and tell yourself why you selected them.

"Choosing my major was one of the most important decisions I've made in college. It's something that will shape the course of my career and my future, so I wanted to make sure I picked something I was truly passionate about. I spent a lot of time researching different fields, talking to professors and professionals, and shadowing people in various jobs. It wasn't an easy decision, but in the end, I knew I had found the perfect major for me."

Sam Jones, college student

Considering the information that emerged from the "what-if" scenario, you now have an idea of what you would like to pursue as a career. So now it is time to consider what academic degree or major aligns with your career trajectory. Here are some tips:

How to select the perfect major

1. Explore your interests:

Consider what you enjoy and are passionate about. Your major does not have to dictate your career, but it should interest you.

2. Research different majors:

Consider different majors, coursework difficulty or challenges, career prospects, and earning potential. Talk to current students, professors, and career counselors to understand what different majors involve.

3. Consider your career goals:

Consider the type of career you want and the majors that align with those goals. Remember that you can change your career path later, but a clear direction can help guide your studies.

4. Open your options:

Take your time to choose a major. Many colleges allow students to explore different subjects before committing to a major. You can also consider double majoring or completing a minor to give yourself more options.

5. Do not be afraid to ask for help.

If you need help deciding on a major, seek help from academic advisors, career counselors, and other resources on campus. They can help you explore your options and make an informed decision.

6. Start with the end in mind!

When you start with the end in mind, you will know the exact steps to get there. This process begins with selecting the correct type of college for your career. Review the first quarter again, where I discussed the different types of colleges. Will your career require a four-year, more traditional route? Could you secure your career path by attending a community college or a technology school?

Choosing the right college is key to your success. Find out what the college is known for, examine previous graduates, and determine if they have been successful in doing what you want.

7. Do not make money the main reason to pick a major or career.

Yes, although money is necessary, it should not be the only reason you select a job. Remember, some miserable millionaires hate waking up and going to work. Select something that you enjoy doing.

8. Conduct preliminary research.

Do more than just apply to college and show up on the first day. Take the time to research the institution and possible majors. Remember, college is a considerable investment. So, you do not want to take it lightly. Tour the school, and stop and ask current students, faculty, and staff questions about their experience while on tour. Do this and thank me later. Set up a meeting with the department dean of your possible major. Introduce yourself and talk about your goals and aspirations. Ask him or her those tough questions, like why students could be more successful in their major. He or she will remember you the entire time you are at the college, and wouldn't it be great if you got a recommendation to graduate school or a scholarship from the dean of the college?

9. Qualifications (What must you obtain to succeed?)

As simple as it sounds, find out what qualifications you need to pursue your dream job successfully. For example, math and science proficiency is necessary if you are trying to become a nurse. Additionally, some jobs require obtaining a master's degree or more. Knowing what qualifications are needed before you decide on a major is essential.

10. Visit the Career Center on campus.

Every institution will have a career center. These centers have personnel, resources, and tools to help you choose the perfect career track.

11. Classes you need to take or major in

Find out what classes you need to take from your professional academic college advisor. Most colleges even have technology and apps that detail your academic trajectory to ensure the timely completion of a degree.

12. Biggest Challenges

If you were driving to an important event and only had 20 minutes to get there and noticed standstill traffic on the expressway upon entry, you would have considered a different route. Apply the same concept to your degree. Find out in advance what challenges lie ahead. Go a different route to avoid wasting time or energy standing still in traffic.

13. Opportunities in Careers

Explore all the careers you seek and research what they offer. I am in education, and there are endless educational opportunities besides teaching. It would take me all day to name them all. However, an internship is a great tool to help you identify a possible career path. Internships are crucial in helping you get on-the-job training. Every student should seek at least an internship while they are in college, as this invaluable experience can help you determine early on if you are on the correct career path.

AN INTRODUCTION TO NETWORKING FOR INTERNS

T he college years are a time for exploration, growth, and self-discovery. However, it is also a great time to learn about yourself, get some experience in your chosen field of study, and build connections to help you succeed in your future career.

In this section, we will talk about some of the best ways for college students to connect with professionals in their field and build their career networks.

First things first: what is networking?

Networking is making connections with people who can help you achieve your goals. It is all about building relationships with people who can open doors for you, whether they are mentors in your field of study or potential employers who might hire you after graduation.

Networking is essential to success at any stage of life. However, it is especially imperative during college because it allows you to explore different paths before committing to one particular career or industry.

Networking is about making friends and connecting with people who share your interests, and discovering what they have achieved.

More than a good degree is needed to secure today's job offer. Solid experience is now just as valuable as your degree when building a successful career. As a result, internships have become an important way to help candidates make themselves stand out.

I remember having my first internship at Channel 5 New Station in Memphis, TN. I majored in communications and knew I would be the next big thing in reporting the news. I was wrong. I thought you wore a suit, smiled, and read the teleprompter. Most news anchors start off reporting news out in the city. They must find, write, and produce unique stories in insufferable weather conditions. Keep in mind that only a few of those journalists make it to the news desk. Very competitive market.

How can I network?

As a college student, you may wonder, "How can I network better?"

It is an important question to ask. Networking is one of the most effective ways for college students to find jobs and internships, and even if you are not looking for a job or internship, networking can help you find people who share your interests and learn more about what you want in life.

How do you get started? Here are six tips for face-to-face networking for interns:

1. Remember names.

When someone introduces themselves to you, double-check the pronunciation of their name and use it in conversation as much as possible. That way, when they introduce themselves again, they will remember that YOU remembered their name! It makes them feel good, which makes you feel good too.

2. Express interest in others' interests.

No one wants to talk with someone who only asks questions about themselves, so ask about other people first! Ask them about their major, hobbies, or anything else that interests them. By doing this, they will feel as though someone is listening to them and is interested in learning about their story, as well as, knowing they have something in common with others.

3. Attend events.

When events are happening on and off campus, make sure you attend them! You never know who might be there waiting for someone like you to come along and introduce yourself.

4. Participate in professional meetings to meet new people.

One of the best ways to network is by attending conferences, workshops, and other professional events. You can make connections at conferences because everyone there is genuinely interested in their work and shares similar values.

5. Share goals with others.

When people know your goals, they will be able to introduce you to others who can help you achieve them. If someone does not seem like someone who could help you, do not be afraid to say thanks—but also do not be afraid to ask questions so that if there is a connection that could benefit both of you, you can make it happen!

6. Understand your contribution to the profession.

When you talk about yourself or your work, you focus on what makes you unique and special—not just another person doing this job or being interested in it because it pays well or looks good on paper.

Online Networking

It can be daunting if you are new to online networking. However, it is pretty straightforward. If you have a LinkedIn profile and a digital portfolio, you have the tools you need to be successful.

Here are some tips for getting started:

1) Manage your image: You want people to see you as an expert in your field. Ensure your LinkedIn profile highlights your relevant skills and includes a professional headshot.

2) Collect recommendations: A recommendation from someone who knows you well can go a long way toward helping other people get to know you better. Ask for them when relevant (e.g., if someone hires or promotes you).

3) Build a digital portfolio: Create a website or blog that showcases your work and experience so others can see what makes you stand out from the crowd! It is also helpful for potential employers or clients who might need to learn more about your profession.

4) Join conversations: When someone posts something interesting in your groups or communities on LinkedIn or Facebook, jump in with an intelligent response!

Networking Conclusion

Networking is one of the most important skills a new professional can develop to secure employment upon graduation. It also helps you find internships and paid jobs at companies where you can learn more about your field and improve your skills.

In-person networking is best because it will enable you to meet people in person and get to know them better. You can also build relationships with other students in your class or program who may not be on your primary career path but may be helpful later. In-person events are also great for meeting potential employers and job recruiters who can help you find an internship or job once you graduate.

Online networking is also essential because some universities may offer few opportunities for students not part of a club or organization on campus. For example, suppose there is no active business club on campus, it might be difficult for students interested in business careers (like accounting) to meet new people and connect with others who share their interests and goals.

Networking and branding are two sides of the same coin. If you are networking, you are trying to build your brand; if you are branding, you are trying to network. So let's talk more about branding.

BRANDING YOURSELF FOR COLLEGE AND BEYOND

B rand management is a topic many college students could learn more about, as it can make a big difference in their lives. It is all about how you present yourself and your work to the world. So what is brand management?

- A set of marketing and communication strategies that set you apart from your competitors and leave a lasting impression on your customers
- A brand's visual identity is the overall look of its communication. Accurately using imagery (fonts, colors, etc.) makes it recognizable.

The first step to brand management is understanding:

- Who are you?
- What do you stand for?
- How do you want people to perceive you?

Once you have an idea of who your brand is, it is time to start establishing it, which means making sure that everything you put out into the world reflects your values. Do your clothes reflect those values? Do you present yourself in a way that shares what makes you special?

One way to do this is by creating a visual identity for yourself. This image can be anything from a logo or tagline for your business to a signature color palette or font style. It helps people identify with the message behind whatever they are looking at and makes them feel connected with something bigger than themselves—which means they will keep coming back.

It takes time to build a brand, but if you are just starting, you do not have to worry about fighting with the rest of the world for attention. College is a time when your brand can grow and develop organically. Focus on building relationships with people around you, getting involved in campus activities, and focusing on what makes YOU different from everyone else.

As you determine who you are and what your brand stands for, examine how these things align with your goals, and do not let anyone tell you they are foolish or impossible.

Brand management is about being true to yourself and knowing what makes you special. I want you to look into this image of a mirror and write down five descriptions you believe your brand represents! What makes you marketable?

1.

2.

3.

4.

5.

Four Steps to Selling/Branding Yourself as the Right Person for the Job

We are all familiar with the importance of personal branding. It is a key component in getting your foot in the door, and it helps you stand out from the crowd.

So how do you do it?

However, first, let us look at what personal branding is not: it is not just about making yourself look good—it is about making yourself useful.

Knowing who you are or what you have to offer can be challenging when starting your career. However, if you can develop valuable and distinct skills, people will take notice.

Here are ways to develop a personal brand as a college student:

1.) Develop Usable Skills: One of the best ways to build a solid personal brand is by developing usable skills. This approach means developing a particular skill set that people need and want—and then honing those skills until they shine through in everything you do.

2.) Be likable: Your personality is as important as your skills in developing an attractive personal brand as a college student. People want to work with people

98

they like, so ensure you are always friendly and kind toward everyone around you.

3.) Craft your story. What makes you unique? What makes you different from everyone else on campus? Your answer should be something that will help potential employers hire you instead of someone with similar qualifications.

4.) Cultivate a positive attitude! It might seem obvious, but it is important: no matter what happens in life and/or at school, always try to see the bright side—even if it means looking outside yourself for inspiration.

5.) Build your online presence. Use your website, social media profiles, and other platforms to build a professional online presence.

6.) Make connections and talk to people: Get to know people in your field or industry and talk to them. This strategy can help you establish yourself as a thought leader and expand your reach.

7.) Consistently showcase your brand: Be consistent in presenting yourself and your brand. This approach includes your appearance, communication style, and the content you share.

8.) Keep an eye on and manage your reputation. Keep an eye on your online presence and professionally deal with negative feedback or reviews.

Developing a personal brand does not just help in the professional world—it can also make it easier to find professionals and acquaintances in college. People want to be around people who are confident, know what they want out of life, and are willing to put in the hard work necessary to achieve their goals. Establishing yourself as someone who knows what they want out of life and is willing to put in the time and effort necessary for success will make it easier for others to relate to you and work with you towards their goals.

SECOND QUARTER RECAP

Choosing a college major is one of the most significant decisions you'll make. It shapes your future, and it can be hard to know where to start. Remember that this is a process. It is not something you do once and then forget about forever—it is something you'll constantly be revisiting as you go through different stages of life.

Do not forget about networking! If there are people in your field who can assist you in securing internships or employment after graduation, reach out to them now—that way, when the time comes for those opportunities, they will already know who you are!

Finally, we touched on brand management for college students. Like the major brands you love, you, too, are a brand. It is essential to begin thinking about it now and executing the strategies outlined so people know who you are and what you represent.

THIRD QUARTER

ACADEMICS

N ow that we have gotten you through the first two quarters of college, it is time to get in gear and drive this thing home.

Let's talk about one of the most critical parts of your college career: academics.

In the next half of the book, you will learn what happens inside the classroom. College students who get this crucial strategy of mastering academics as if it were an actual job will win every time.

In high school, I remember signing up for every 8 a.m. class, and I had to be there at 7 a.m.   I followed a similar strategy my first year of college because I lived on campus, and sometimes classes were right next door, and I enrolled in classes taught on Fridays.

Boy, did I not have a clue!

I remember being late every other day to the morning class. After my third tardiness, a professor pulled me aside and said,

"Sir, you have one more time to interrupt my class, and the consequence will be a letter grade dropped off your final grade."

He also instructed me to check the syllabus, which I had never looked at; you might see a common theme here. I was unprepared for how I scheduled my classes and when I planned my classes without looking at the bible of the course, i.e., the syllabi.

Academics in college are important because they form the foundation of your college education. Your grades and coursework will not only reflect your knowledge and understanding of the subject matter but will also play a role in determining your future academic and career opportunities.

Good grades can lead to options such as scholarships, internships, and graduate school admissions. They can also give you an advantage when applying for jobs after college.

The skills and knowledge you gain from your college courses will be valuable in your personal and professional lives. Employers value skills like critical thinking, problem-solving, and communication, which you can learn in college.

Overall, getting good grades in college is important because it sets you up for future academic and career success. It is important to prioritize your academics and make the necessary effort to succeed. The first tip is time management.

TIME MANAGEMENT SKILLS

"I wasn't very good at managing my time in college at first. I would procrastinate on assignments, stay up late, and struggle to balance my coursework with extracurricular activities and a part-time job. It was overwhelming, and I started to feel burnt out. Eventually, I learned the importance of time management and started using a planner to organize my schedule and prioritize my tasks. It made a huge difference and helped me be more productive and successful in college."

Tyler Hampton, College Student

So, what is time management?

Time is the one thing you cannot ever get back! If you can master this skill, this mastery alone will get you to the finish line when you get to college. In your college classes, punctuality is almost more important than the content you learn. The main tip is to treat your classes like a job. Suppose your shift starts at 8 a.m. You are penalized if you are late;

remember, after a certain amount of tardiness, you will soon get terminated. Most professors will not take attendance. However, they are watching and will not take you seriously as a professional student based on your actions.

As a student, learning how to manage your time is important because it can help you keep track of all your responsibilities and decide what to do first. It can also help you reduce stress and avoid feeling overwhelmed.

Here are some reasons why managing your time is important for students:

1. You have limited time.
   As a student, you likely have many demands on your time, including classes, assignments, exams, extracurricular activities, and possibly even a part-time job. Managing your time can help you make the most of it.
2. You need to prioritize your tasks:
   By managing your time, you can prioritize your tasks and focus on the most important ones first. This management can help you stay on track and avoid falling behind.
3. You can reduce stress.
   When juggling multiple responsibilities, it can be easy to feel overwhelmed. By managing your time effectively, you can reduce stress and feel more in control of your schedule.

4. You can improve your academic performance.
   Managing your time can help you allocate enough time for studying and completing assignments. This strategy can lead to improved grades and academic success.

Time management is a crucial part of any task; you must master this skill now in college. It is essential to ensure you have enough time to complete tasks and reach your goals, but it can be difficult if you do not know how much time you have to work on each task.

When scheduling your time, it is important to consider your available time for tasks and how long it will take to complete them. While some tasks might only take an hour or two, others may require weeks or months of work. You'll want to plan so that you can handle the amount of time needed to achieve something.

You should also consider what types of tasks need to be completed first. For example, if you are working on a project that requires multiple steps before completion, those steps should be scheduled at the beginning rather than later when needed. This way, there is a chance of remembering all steps along the way!

The Code to Time Management

First, create a semester calendar. This calendar will help you see how much time you have set aside for class and how much time is left over for other things.

A big part of time management is setting priorities. You will want to set your personal goals and then figure out what needs prioritization first to reach them. Ensure your preferences are realistic and do not burn yourself out by trying to do too much at once!

Another essential aspect to consider is distinguishing wants from needs. This separation can be challenging because sometimes we convince ourselves that we need more than we do! If you feel stressed about social outings or spending money on entertainment instead of saving up for a rainy day, look first at what is essential in your life. Then make sure that those things are getting the attention they deserve!

Finally, balance work and play so you do not get burned out from stress or boredom! This balance might mean taking breaks from studying every hour or two to stay energized before reaching any breakthroughs in understanding concepts.

Remember, procrastination is a common issue for college students, who are often overwhelmed by the work they must do. Many students find themselves in a cycle of putting off tasks until the last minute and then scrambling to get them done. So let's dive deeper:

List 5 reasons you procrastinate:

1.

2.

3.

4.

5.

Now, those same five reasons you listed, what five ways can you overcome these behaviors?

1.

2.

3.

4.

5.

OVERCOMING PROCRASTINATION

It is easier than you think. Here are five simple steps to start:

- Make the task meaningful.
  What does this mean? It means that you should find a way to connect your current project with something you care about. It could be something external, like a relationship, or internal, like your self-esteem. If you are passionate about the project and its outcome, you are more likely to see it through rather than allow yourself to become distracted.
- Break the project down into smaller steps.
  This process will help you feel like you are making progress on your goal, even in small amounts at once. If a task seems overwhelming, try setting aside just five minutes daily to work on it—you might be surprised at how quickly those five minutes add up!
- Keep yourself organized!

When we are overwhelmed or stressed out by our workloads, we can fall into the trap of thinking that if we just keep everything together in one big pile on our desks, everything will magically get done on time and meet everyone's expectations, but that is not true! You need a system so that you know where to start when things get out of hand.

- Finally, plan a reward for when you finish each step in your project.
  This reward could be anything from going out with friends after completing an assignment at school to indulging in a new book on Audible! The key is to ensure that your reward is something positive that will give you energy and motivation to complete those last few steps (and remember: no matter how small or large those final steps may seem—they are pretty big!).
- Take action today! You will no longer have to think about the task when you complete it.

Now that you have several strategies to combat issues around time management, let us talk about learning and conquering the content while you are in the class.

HOW TO PASS EVERY CLASS WITH FLYING COLORS.

⌒⌒⌒⌒

F irst, look ahead before class: This means dissecting each part of your class syllabus. I like to refer to this as the bible of the course. It will give you everything you need to know about the class, including the days and times you meet, the professor's contact information, the goals of the course, and learning outcomes. The most important part of the syllabus is that it will give you the breakdown of your final grade for the course. Here is an example:

Example

Class Participation: 10 percent

3 Tests: 20 percent each.

Attendance: 30 percent.

So, if you miss half of the classes, the highest grade you may earn is an 85 in the class. Hopefully, you recognize the importance of reviewing the class syllabus to determine your progress in the course.

Although this pertinent information is in the syllabus, you will be surprised how many students never review the syllabus. If they do, it is in the bottom of their backpacks, never to be brought out again.

Do not let that be you!

Do the assigned reading if your professor assigns it. I promise you will see it again in a writing assignment or on the quiz. Do not assume it will not surface again because it was not discussed in class.

Communicate with your professor like a pro!

The most common thing I hear from professors about students is that communication is typically initiated during finals as students explore opportunities for extra credit.

So, I am telling you now: do not wait until finals to communicate with your professor.

Check the course syllabus, find out the professor's office hours and how to reach them, and make it your top priority to meet with your professor before finals! This forward movement will set the tone for you as a professional student in that class. It could be simple. Here is an example below.

Hello, my name is _____, and I'm from _____.

I'm excited about your class; list why you are excited.

I'm nervous about your course and list the reasons why.

With this simple introduction, your professor will know who you are and assist you in succeeding in the course because you are committed to doing the necessary work. Now, don't just stop by that one time; make it part of your goals to stop by at least twice that semester to check in with your professor.

In between office visits, emails are the standard form of communication with professors. Over the years, I have noticed that many students need help writing professional emails. Learning how to write a professional email will take you far and, more importantly, will determine how others respond to you and your request.

Here are a few quick tips.

- Use your college email address when it is about college business. If you use a personal email address, ensure it has a professional username. Preferably your first and last name.
- Include the following in the email:

- Start with a greeting, such as, (Hello, Greetings, good morning, good afternoon.) Professor's Title and Last Name
- The opening line is usually positive: "I hope all is well your way." or "happy holidays."
- A brief reminder of how they know you: "I take your English 1010 class on Monday at 10:00 am."
- Then get to the point—tell them why you are writing them. Try to keep this short. Remember, they have limited time and have more things to do besides reading emails. Remember, too, to keep this request positive.
- Closing
- Your name and contact information

You must read your email before sending. I suggest asking a close friend to review it to ensure they understand your request. Also, emails are usually the first means of communication, so it is important to identify spelling or grammar errors. Learning this skill is critical to your success as a professional student, whether with your professors, advisors, financial aid office, or club advisor.

REMOVE DISTRACTIONS.

O ne of the easiest ways to get off track is to allow distractions to become a priority.

Most college students have more free time.

Well, it seemed that way at the beginning. Parents are not there to monitor your whereabouts. Do not get me wrong. I had a great time in college, attending the Kappa parties and homecoming festivities, and the list continues. However, I could only participate in some of them.

Sometimes I had to put my classwork first to remain in college. Most students in college have to maintain a certain GPA to maintain their scholarship or even to be involved in on-campus activities or organizations; you must maintain a certain GPA. College athletes, in particular, have to monitor their GPA to maintain eligibility.

Here are a few tips to help you minimize those distractions.

Write your distractions out. List them here, whether it is spending too much time on social media or watching too much television. Put them down. That is the only way you will know how to avoid those pitfalls if you recognize what they are.

Next, develop a plan so the distractions you listed above will not harm you in the future.

For example, if you listed television as one of your distractions, tell yourself how you plan to overcome it. Limit yourself to watching television only on the weekends. If that is too extreme, watch TV only after you complete your studies and homework.

How does that sound? Ok, have at it. Write out that plan below!

Who do you have as your accountability team? Who can you share your distractions with, and who would like to keep you accountable?

1.

2.

3.

4.

5.

Having accountability partners is critical in helping you make the touchdown in the classroom. Surround yourself with LIKE-minded people.

LEARNING STYLES

The term learning style is a technique used to describe how people gather, interpret, organize, come to conclusions, and store new information. Learning styles are often categorized by sensory approaches, with the most popular learning styles being visual, auditory, and kinesthetic.

Listen to me!

If you recognize how you take in information, process it, and interpret it early in your college career, you will be steps ahead of most; keep that in mind. Knowing your learning style can be helpful in the classroom because it can help you understand how you learn best and tailor your study habits accordingly. There are several learning styles: visual, auditory, reading/writing, and kinesthetic, and I will provide more information on the following pages.

Here are some ways that knowing your learning style can help you in the classroom:

- You can tailor your study habits to your learning style:
  By understanding your learning style, you can tailor your study habits to match your

strengths. For example, if you are a visual learner, you might benefit from using mind maps or diagrams to study. In contrast, an auditory learner might find it helpful to listen to lectures or review material out loud.

- You can communicate your needs to your instructors:
  Knowing your learning style can also help you express your needs to your instructors. If you have a specific learning style, you can let your instructors know so they can tailor their teaching style to meet your needs better.
- You can maximize your study time
  by understanding your learning style and focusing on the most effective activities. This information can help you remember things better and save time by letting you avoid studying methods that do not work for you.

If you know how you learn best, you can change how you study, tell your teachers what you need, and make the most of your study time. Implementing these strategies can improve academic performance and create a more enjoyable learning experience. We learn best when pieces of information are presented to us in a way that caters to our preferred learning style. Below, I explain the three most popular learning styles. See which one might fit you.

Visual Learners

Characteristics	Study Strategies
• Take detailed notes. • Sit in front of the class. • Close their eyes to visualize something. • Benefit from illustrations and colorful presentations. • Watch the professor's body language and facial expression to help understand the lecture. • Prefer professors who are dramatic and dynamic. • Prefer to study alone in a quiet place.	• Convert your lecture notes into a visual format (picture, chart, graph, symbol, diagram, map). • Write notes with different colors. • Put complex concepts or processes into flow charts or timelines.

Auditory Learners

Characteristics	Study Strategies
• Listen to the tone of voice, pitch, speed, etc. to interpret the content of lectures and talk concepts through • Sit where they can hear the professor. • Hum or talk to themselves. • Acquire knowledge by reading aloud. • Listen to tape-recorded books or lectures. • Prefer studying in groups to studying alone.	• Use a tape recorder in class. • Attend all class lectures. • Take note of examples, stories, and jokes during lectures. • Read your notes and textbooks aloud. • Realize that your notes may be lacking due to your focus on listening. Compare notes with other students.

Kinesthetic Learners	
Characteristics	Study Strategies
• Prefer hands-on courses. • It is challenging to sit still for long periods. • Sit near the door or somewhere they can quickly move around. • You communicate by touching and gesturing. • Prefers study groups or creating projects.	• Take notes in lectures. • Retype your notes on a computer. • Create flashcards for concepts with precisely sequential information. • Try to utilize case studies that make the concepts "more real" for you. • Create projects that allow you to utilize your senses. • Take a course that requires labs, projects, and hands-on experiments.

Now that you have read through each learning style, which learner are you?

Below, list every class and what type of professor you have in each class. Next, list some tips you learned above based on your learning style.

HOW TO SELECT THE RIGHT PROFESSORS

1. Check out ratemyprofessor.com. This site will give you a glimpse of what other students say about the professor.
2. Look for online video courses. Many professors upload their lectures on YouTube. Take a few minutes to listen and see if their lecture style fits your learning style, as you learned above.
3. Check out the professor's course website or blog.
4. Find past or current students attending or graduating from your college, and ask which professors should take and professors that are challenging.
5. Read the professor's published work. Many professors are published authors, so reading their work allows you to learn more about their professional stance on specific issues.
6. Sit in on some classes. When you tour the college, ask the staff outside the general tour if you could visit the academic department.

7. Trial and error: Some professors you will have to experience to know if their style works for you.

THIRD QUARTER RECAP

We have covered a lot, but college is a whirlwind of new experiences. You will learn new things, meet new people, and try new activities, which is why mastering time management in college is so important. First, do not let yourself get overwhelmed by all the work. If you do not have enough time in the day, it is okay. You can always make up for it later and follow the strategies I offered.

Second, try not to procrastinate too much! It can be tempting to put off work until later because it seems like there is not enough time right now, but there will always be more work coming up soon enough! Just do what you can as quickly as possible rather than waiting until the last minute and stressing about it later.

Remember that talking to your professors is important to get along with them and ensure they know how hard you worked on their assignments. Also, finding out what learning style works best for you is essential. This information will help you succeed in class and life.

Finally, selecting professors who will work well with your learning style and help you succeed in college is essential.

FOURTH QUARTER

FINANCING YOUR EDUCATION

I do not know your financial situation, but my parents forgot to create this magic college fund for me. So, I needed all the available financial aid to attend college. College is expensive, and I will not pretend it is not. However, college is an investment in yourself. For example, the average college graduate is 24 percent more likely to be employed than non-graduates, and average earnings among graduates are $32,000 annually and $1.2 million higher over a lifetime.

Show me the money!

Let's break this down even more:

- Men with bachelor's degrees make about $900,000 more over their lifetimes than men with just a high school diploma.
- Women with bachelor's degrees earn $630,000 more than high school graduates.

Paying for college can be a daunting task, as the cost of tuition and other expenses quickly accumulate.

However, many options are available regarding financial assistance for college so that you can achieve your academic goals. Before I provide helpful tips to help you and your family consider the various financing options, let us explore some critical financial aid terms. I learned from many years in higher education that financial aid terms can sound like another language, so I will clarify these terms.

1.) Financial aid

Financial aid is money to pay college-related fees and expenses. It is available from the federal government, state governments, colleges and universities, and even private organizations like banks or employers.

2.) Pell Grants and State Grants

Grants are awards that do not require repayment. These funds are typically awarded based on financial need, although some colleges have "merit-based" grants that do not factor in financial need. You must complete the Free Application for Federal Student Aid (FAFSA) if you apply for federal grants and scholarships. Federal Pell Grants provide up to $5,815 annually for undergraduate students who demonstrate financial need. You can apply online at fafsa.ed.gov and receive an award letter within weeks of submitting your application.

State grants differ from state to state, but they can help pay for tuition, books and supplies, transportation, or living costs while attending full- or part-time school. Since each college has guidelines for awarding money to deserving applicants, the financial aid office typically handles this money. However, some states offer more money.

3.) Subsidized and Unsubsidized Loans

Loans can be an excellent way for students to pay for college because they allow them to defer paying back their loans until after graduation, when their income increases significantly. However, loans come with interest rates that add up over time, so securing what you need and making payments to lower your balance as quickly as possible are essential.

4.) Private scholarships

Organizations, often foundations and nonprofits, award private scholarships. You should apply for as many private scholarships as possible because many do not have any strings attached, and the funds are accepted at any institution you choose.

5.) Employment/Work-study

The third way to fund your college education is by getting a job while in school or working over the summer break (or both). Student employment can come in many forms: work study, which pays you based on hours worked, and internships that provide on-the-job training. Part-time jobs outside the campus are another option if they do not overlap with coursework and other obligations.

6.) Award Letter

When you apply for financial aid, you will receive an award letter from each school you apply to for admission. This letter states the amount you will receive in grants and loans and the specific requirements for receiving those funds. For example, if a school requires that students maintain a certain GPA or GPA range (such as 3.0 or higher), those who do not meet the requirement may not receive any financial aid.

7.) Cost of Attendance

The cost of attendance is the total cost of attending an institution, including tuition, fees, and other expenses like books, supplies, and room and board (if needed). This amount will vary depending on your school's location in the United States and the degree program.

Final Thoughts

It is important to research and understand your options before deciding how to finance your education. One option is financial aid, which may consist of the following forms of aid discussed above: grants, scholarships, and loans. Grants and scholarships are forms of financial aid that do not require repayment, while loans are a form of aid that requires repayment. To determine if you qualify for financial aid, complete and submit the Free Application for Federal Student Aid (FAFSA) and explore other financial aid resources such as private scholarships and grants.

Even if your family makes too much money, you should still complete the FAFSA. Some schools will only offer merit scholarships to students who have completed the FAFSA. The other reason to complete the FAFSA is in the unfortunate case that something happens to the breadwinning parent and family incomes change dramatically.

College is expensive, and determining how you will finance your education can be overwhelming. However, do not let fear of the cost stop you from attending college! There are many different ways to fund your education, and almost every student receives some financial aid.

Before we close this section, remember that free money does not come with an interest rate.

Be careful of scholarship awards that are packed with loans. I advise you to take the time before you agree to accept any scholarship to know everything included in the package. I have worked with many students who thought their scholarship package was free, but that was different. The institution gave them

$10,000 in free scholarship money but paired it with a $20,000 loan. So, it looked to be a full ride. However, it was not. So to sum this up, read and understand everything you sign! If you do not know, ask questions!

Overall, paying for college is a significant investment, but many options are available to help you cover the cost. By exploring financial aid, working while in college, and considering alternative payment options, you can find a solution that works for you.

FINANCIAL AID: CALCULATING EXPENSES

A s noted in the previous section for parents and students, college costs can get expensive, and after applying for financial aid for school, you and your student will see many expenses accumulate. So looking at these expenses will prepare your college student for the real world and allow them to experience the impact of their actions on their finances. The following breakdown will be very helpful to you, as it will estimate the cost of attendance per semester and for the year. The Cost of Attendance table is a great tool for planning and preparing for anticipated expenses.

Only fill in yellow cells;		
College Costs	Semester	Year
Tuition		
Fees	$ -	$ -

138

Room	$ -	$ -
Board	$ -	$ -
Miscellaneous - Add all (books, trans., etc.)	$ -	$ -
Total Costs	$ -	$ -
	$ -	$ -

Grants and Scholarships

College Grants/Scholarships		
Pell		$ -
SEOG	$ -	$ -
State Scholarships	$ -	$ -
Other Grants/Scholarships	$ -	$ -
Other Grants/Scholarships	$ -	$ -
Other Grants/Scholarships	$ -	$ -

Grant Total	$ -		$ -
	$ -		$ -
Loans			
Sub Stafford			
Unsub Stafford	$ -		$ -
Perkins	$ -		$ -
PLUS	$ -		$ -
Loan Total	$ -		$ -
	$ -		$ -
Costs			
Bill from the College			
Miscellaneous Expenses (not included in the bill)	$ -		$ -
	$ -		$ -
Total Estimated Costs			

Cost if you didn't take a Loan	$ -		$ -
	$ -		$ -

Work Study

Work Study can be cash to the student or used to pay the bill. Only include this if you plan to use work study to pay the bill.			
			$ -
Cost minus All Aid including Work Study			
	$ -		$ -
Standard Payment Plan Estimate 25% (4 payments per sem)			
Payment Plan Estimate 25% (4 payments per sem) No Loan	$ -		
Payment Plan Estimate 25% (4 payments per sem) Loan and Work Study included	$ -		
	$ -		

The Cost of Attendance sheet is a great way to determine the cost to attend different schools. Here are a couple of reasons you should compare schools.

There are several reasons why comparing the cost of colleges is essential:

1. Costs can vary widely.
   College tuition and other costs can vary greatly, even between schools offering the same programs. By comparing the cost of different colleges, you can better understand what you can afford and find a school that fits your budget.
2. Financial aid can affect the net cost:
   The cost of attendance at a college is not always the same as the net cost, which is the amount you pay after financial aid is taken into account. By comparing the net costs of different colleges, you can get a more accurate picture of what you will pay.
3. Different colleges may offer different financial aid packages:
   These can vary significantly. By comparing the costs of colleges and the financial aid packages they offer, you can find a school that provides the best financial fit for you.
4. You may be able to negotiate:
   If more than one college gives you money to cover expenses and fees, you may be able to negotiate with them for more money. By

comparing the cost and financial aid packages different schools offer, you can determine which ones may be willing to negotiate. Overall, it is essential to compare the costs of colleges to find a school that fits your budget and offers the best financial aid package. This comparison can help you make an informed decision about where to attend college.

- Other things to think about when considering the cost of attending a school are.

- Living at home or on campus?

- Transportation to and from campus and also to and from home.

- Food (Meal plans and Groceries),

- Clothes,

- Toiletry Items,

- Social Activities,

- Books

- Technology Codes.

- Do you see where I am going? ☺

- Consider all of these costs when selecting a college.

ASK FOR MORE MONEY!

Earlier, I mentioned private scholarships and grants, as many organizations, foundations, and nonprofits give free money to aspiring college students. If you want to apply for a private scholarship or grant, you may need to write an essay or letter. Also, when applying for additional funds, remember the following:

- Tell your story of why you need the money.
- If you are from a single-parent home, are a first-generation college student, or have a parent who lost a job, you may want to discuss this experience.
- Be prepared to request support from others as references, as some scholarships will request a letter of recommendation.

Listed below is a sample letter you can reference for your scholarship application.

Sample Letter:

As a student, paying for college can be a significant financial burden. I have already taken out loans and

144

applied for scholarships to cover my tuition and living expenses, but I still struggle to make ends meet. I am writing to request additional financial assistance to help me afford the cost of college.

I understand that many other students are also in need of financial support. Still, I hope you will consider my situation and that I am working hard to succeed academically. I have a 3.7 GPA and participate in several extracurricular activities on campus. I am committed to making the most of my college experience. I believe that receiving additional financial assistance will enable me to focus on my studies and not worry about how I will pay for my education.

I would appreciate any extra money you could give me so I can keep going to school. Thank you for considering my request.

FINANCIAL TIPS FOR YOUR COLLEGE STUDENT

P arents, if you have a son or daughter in college right now or a teenager planning to attend a university soon, you are probably hoping and praying they have the necessary skills to manage their money. Why not ensure they know a few significant financial tips before they leave home? These tips will help.

Learning to monitor money with a checking account

Having a checking account is a big responsibility and an excellent opportunity for your young adult to learn how to keep track of how much money they spend. Learning to monitor money is essential for your college student. Although prepaid credit cards may be convenient, financial education regarding usage is minimum. However, if they have a checking account, they must watch their balance and take care of expenses.

Learning to monitor spending now

A college student needs awareness to develop his methods of reducing expenses. For example, rather than eating lunch out every day, he could pack a lunch. He could purchase groceries and meal prep, so we can reduce the expenses he may spend on eating out.

Setting aside funds for entertainment

Sure, college is a blast. Still, your student must see the importance of planning a finite amount of money for having fun rather than spending cash frivolously on going to the movies, eating out with friends, and traveling with friends.

"I quickly learned that one of the biggest expenses in college was textbooks. I started renting my textbooks whenever possible, buying used books, and sharing them with friends to save money. It was a little extra effort, but it paid off in the long run. By the end of my college career, I had saved hundreds of dollars on textbooks."

Nikki Brown, college student

Shh, here are five tips below to help you save!

1. Share textbooks with classmates.
   If you feel comfortable with this process and know the student, split the textbook expense with another student. Additionally, you gain a study buddy in the process.

2. The Library
   Yes, most libraries buy a copy to hold in the library for each class offered at that college. Most libraries allow their students to use them in the library for FREE! How can you lose? You are in the library and can simultaneously check out the books you need for free. Many libraries keep copies of frequently assigned textbooks in stock. However, you may compete against other students reading this book, so get there early.

3. Rent your textbooks.
   Companies often rent textbooks, and this can be less expensive than purchasing books from Amazon, Valore, CampusBooks, and several other retailers that offer textbook rentals.

4. Go Beyond the Campus Bookstore:
   Yes, I said it! Although they include the campus bookstore on your college tour and give you a fancy t-shirt, do your research. In some cities, there are multiple bookstores

outside the campus, so price check. Remember, your ultimate goal is to save all the money you can.

5. Access Codes

Keep this on the down low, but many books now offer access codes at an additional cost. You can opt out of many of those codes if you do not need them. They can save you a lot of money if you opt-out. Now, it is always wise to ask your professor before you opt out of them. Some require you to have them do specific assignments or quizzes for the course.

Congratulations!

You have unlocked all the secrets to getting cheaper books. So, now that you have your textbooks, make sure you use them!

FOURTH QUARTER
RECAP

F inancial aid is the optimal financial tool to help you pay for school, and since you are planning on attending college, you should look into financial aid for college. There are many places to get financial help, like the federal government and your state government. You can also secure financial aid assistance from private organizations and your school.

Remember how I mentioned that financial aid comes in many forms and can be used differently? It can be used to pay tuition, books, housing costs, and other expenses associated with attending school. The different types of financial aid include grants, scholarships, and loans. Grants are free money that does not have to be repaid, while loans require repayment with interest after graduation. Scholarships are also free but vary in terms of what they cover (some may only cover tuition while others may cover everything).

The best strategy to learn about financial aid programs is to visit your local high school guidance office or public library. They will have information on all types of financial aid programs, scholarships, and grants that could help pay for college expenses like books or transportation costs if needed!

Finally, now that you have the money, you must learn to manage it. Do not forget to review my tips on managing a checking account and other savvy ways to save money.

FINAL SCORE: YOU GRADUATE!

In the United States, college is a rite of passage. It is a time to pursue your degree and start your career, and it is also a time to make lifelong friends and build an identity for yourself.

College is an exciting time. You are entering a new world, making new friends, and learning about yourself. It is also a stressful time. You have classes, homework, extracurriculars, and maybe even a job or internship, all while trying to figure out who you are and what your place in the world will be.

Being a successful college student requires more than just good grades. It requires dedication, hard work, and time management. It involves setting clear goals, prioritizing responsibilities, and seeking help when needed. To succeed, you should also be willing to take risks and try new things; these will help you grow and learn.

You should also take care of your mental health by talking to people who understand what you are going through, like other students or professors. This step can help you stay motivated and focused on what matters most: your education!

I hope this book showed you that preparing for college is never too early. Whether you are a freshman in high school or a junior at the end of your first year, there are things you can do now to ensure that college goes smoothly and that you come out with the most from it as possible. If you are thinking about these things now, you can hit the ground running when it comes time to go to school.

ABOUT THE AUTHOR

Meet Dr. Shawn Boyd. When one discovers their passion in life, their purpose for living manifests. A passion for teaching, motivating, and helping students paved the way for Dr. Shawn A. Boyd to emerge quickly as one of the most sought-after motivational speakers in the country. Shawn has traveled and spoken at various colleges around the country.

This college professor is also a podcast host, author, columnist, husband, father, and scholar. He uses his 14 years of leadership experience to connect with audiences worldwide. Whether in front of a classroom or podium, Dr. Boyd uses his expertise to help thousands of students transition from school to the boardroom and has helped scores of professionals achieve success in their work lives. Shawn has worked in many different areas of higher education throughout his career, such as academic advising, student affairs, and admissions. He is known for caring about the success of his students and being able to build solid, helpful relationships with them.

As a certified professional speaker, Dr. Boyd is known for his wit, charm, and razor-sharp insights. He welcomes the opportunity to share his expertise with any organization, group, or individual. Shawn has spoken at many colleges, such as UT Knoxville, Tennessee State University, Austin Peay State University, UT Martin, the University of Memphis, and LeMoyne-Owen College. He has been the keynote speaker at several programs and graduations.

Dr. Boyd is involved in many civic and community non-profit groups, such as the MPLOY Summer Initiative, Shelby County Schools Project STAND, and Kappa Alpha Psi Fraternity, Inc. Dr. Boyd has won awards for his work in the community, such as The Urban Elite's Top 40 Under 40, Leadership Memphis, and the Martin Luther King Jr. Dreamers of Tomorrow award.

To learn more about Dr. Shawn Boyd, please visit his website at www.drshawnboyd.com.

Made in United States
Orlando, FL
07 April 2023